The Learning Works

California Geodoodles

Learning About California Through Step-By-Step Drawings

Grades 3–6

Written by Linda Schwartz • Illustrated by Bev Armstrong

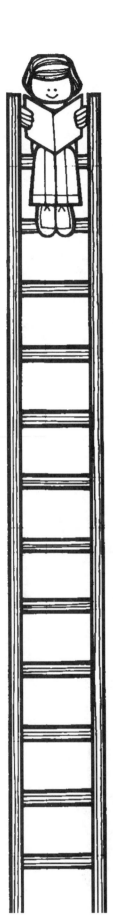

The Learning Works

Typesetting and Editorial Production:
Clark Editorial & Design

Back Cover Art:
Elizabeth Siegel

Special thanks to the students in Mrs. Barbara Barr's fourth-grade class at Roosevelt Elementary School in Santa Barbara, CA.

Copyright © 2000
The Learning Works, Inc.
P.O. Box 6187
Santa Barbara, California 93160

ISBN: 0-88160-355-4
LW 394

Printed in the United States of America.

About California Geodoodles

What better way to learn about California than through drawing! *California Geodoodles* present more than forty high-interest topics about California's history, landmarks, symbols, animals, plants, businesses, sports, recreation, and special events.

For each topic, kids are given step-by-step drawing instructions to follow on their own while drawing on white art paper. Geodoodles are great for visual perception because kids have to determine what has been added in each drawing. Once they've completed the drawings a few times, kids take off on their own and add their own embellishments. Each topic also includes fascinating facts so kids learn about California as they learn how to draw. There is also a map of California, facts in brief, a historical time line, clip art, a list of creative ways to use *California Geodoodles,* and a page of California decorative borders.

California Geodoodles are great for a classroom study of California, to tuck in a backpack when vacationing in the "Golden State," or for fun any time or anywhere.

> **A Note to Students**
> As you follow the steps on separate art paper, draw in pencil. Dotted lines appear in some steps. Make these lines light so that they can be easily erased later. Finish your drawing by going over it with colored pencils, crayons, or felt-tipped pens.

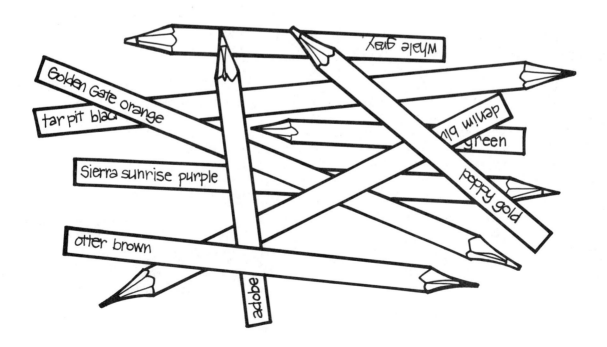

Contents

Map of California

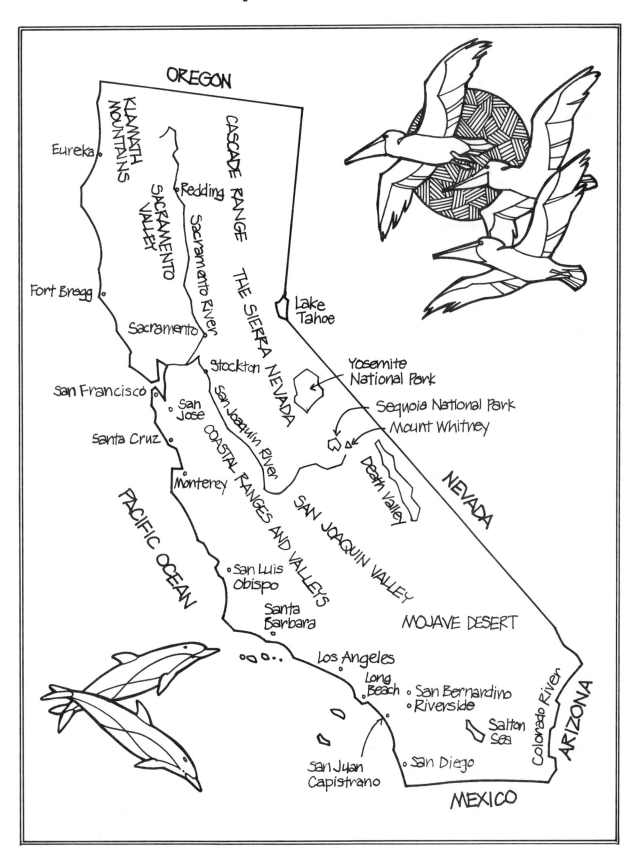

OREGON

KLAMATH MOUNTAINS

Eureka

CASCADE RANGE

Redding

SACRAMENTO VALLEY

Sacramento River

THE SIERRA NEVADA

Fort Bragg

Sacramento

Lake Tahoe

Stockton

Yosemite National Park

San Francisco

San Jose

San Joaquin River

Sequoia National Park

Mount Whitney

Santa Cruz

COASTAL RANGES AND VALLEYS

Monterey

Death Valley

NEVADA

PACIFIC OCEAN

SAN JOAQUIN VALLEY

San Luis Obispo

Santa Barbara

MOJAVE DESERT

Los Angeles

Long Beach

San Bernardino

Riverside

Colorado River

Salton Sea

ARIZONA

San Juan Capistrano

San Diego

MEXICO

5

California Facts in Brief

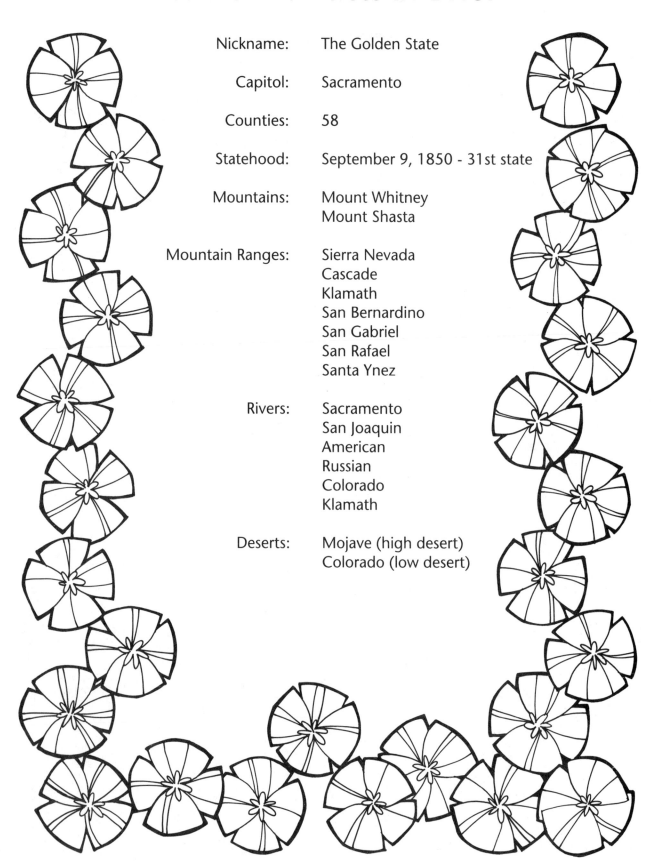

Nickname:	The Golden State
Capitol:	Sacramento
Counties:	58
Statehood:	September 9, 1850 - 31st state
Mountains:	Mount Whitney
	Mount Shasta
Mountain Ranges:	Sierra Nevada
	Cascade
	Klamath
	San Bernardino
	San Gabriel
	San Rafael
	Santa Ynez
Rivers:	Sacramento
	San Joaquin
	American
	Russian
	Colorado
	Klamath
Deserts:	Mojave (high desert)
	Colorado (low desert)

California Facts in Brief

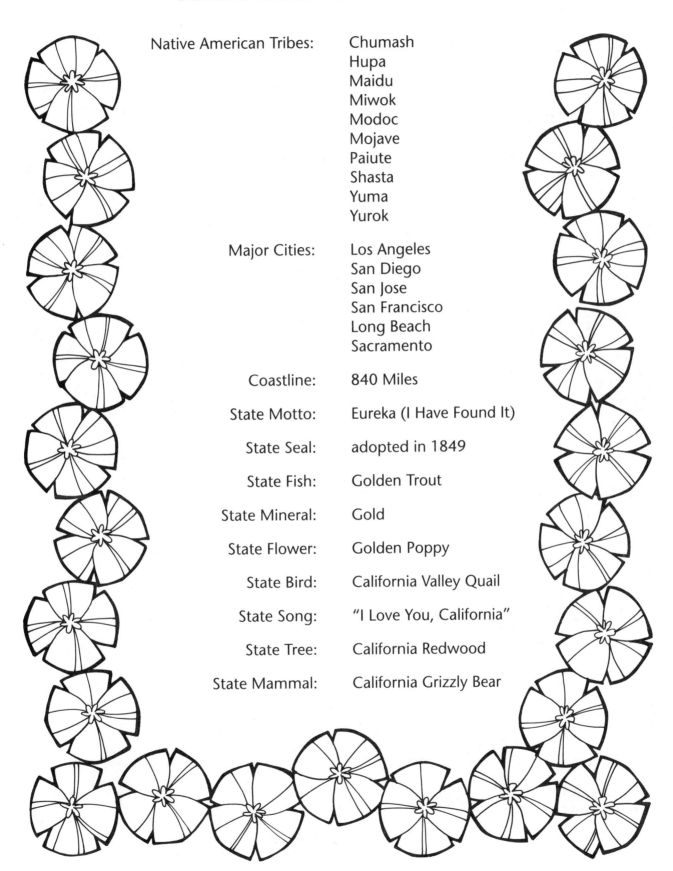

Native American Tribes:	Chumash
	Hupa
	Maidu
	Miwok
	Modoc
	Mojave
	Paiute
	Shasta
	Yuma
	Yurok
Major Cities:	Los Angeles
	San Diego
	San Jose
	San Francisco
	Long Beach
	Sacramento
Coastline:	840 Miles
State Motto:	Eureka (I Have Found It)
State Seal:	adopted in 1849
State Fish:	Golden Trout
State Mineral:	Gold
State Flower:	Golden Poppy
State Bird:	California Valley Quail
State Song:	"I Love You, California"
State Tree:	California Redwood
State Mammal:	California Grizzly Bear

7

Historical Time Line of California

1542   Spanish explorer Juan Rodríguez Cabrillo explores San Diego Bay

1579   Sir Francis Drake lands on the northern California coast and claims the land for England

1769   San Diego is founded; Franciscan priest Junípero Serra begins San Diego de Alcala, the first of twenty-one missions

1776   San Francisco is founded

1781   Los Angeles is founded

1822   California becomes part of Mexico, which had recently won its independence from Spain

1826   Jedediah Smith journeys west to California by land

1842   John C. Fremont leads United States expeditions into California

1848   the Americans win the Mexican War and California is given to the United States

James Marshall discovers gold at Sutter's Mill

1849   the start of the California gold rush

1850   California becomes the 31st state on September 9th

1854   Sacramento is designated as the state's permanent capital

1860   the Pony Express is established linking California to the East

1861   the telegraph reaches California

1869   the first transcontinental railroad system is completed that connects Sacramento to the eastern United States

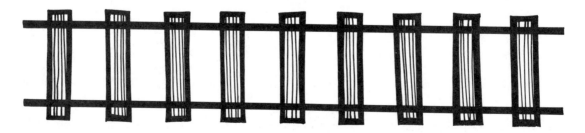

Historical Time Line of California

1890   Yosemite National Park is established

1892   oil is discovered in Los Angeles

1906   the great San Francisco earthquake and fire

1911   women get the right to vote in elections

1913   Los Angeles aqueduct is finished

1927   first movie with sound ("talkie") is made in Los Angeles

1937   The Golden Gate Bridge is completed

1953   Earl Warren, governor of California, becomes chief justice of the United States Supreme Court

1969   Richard M. Nixon of California becomes the thirty- seventh president of the United States

1981   Ronald Reagan of California becomes the fortieth president of the United States

1990   the population of California reaches a new record - 29,760,021

1994   an area north of Los Angeles is hit with an earthquake measuring 6.6 on the Richter scale killing 57 people and causing more than $20 billion in damages

California Clip Art

SUNNY DAY ORANGES

History

Miwok Home

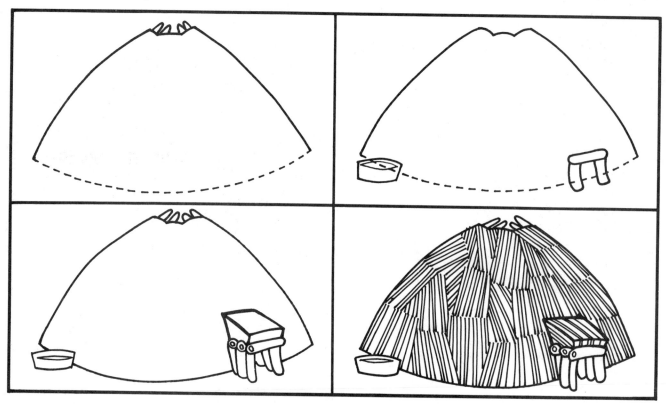

Finishing Touches

Draw smoke from a cooking fire coming up through the hole in the roof of your Miwok home. Miwoks ate acorns. Add an oak tree to your picture.

Fascinating Facts

• Miwok Indians lived in villages of round-topped houses found in the area of Marin County, California and northward to Bodega Bay.

• The houses were wooden-framed structures covered with reeds or redwood bark slabs and built over a depression dug in the ground. In the center of some Miwok villages was a roundhouse, a large community house where members of the tribe gathered.

• In the Miwok home, women wove baskets from reeds that grew along the river. They often decorated these baskets with quail feathers and shells. The women used the baskets for many things including gathering acorns, the main staple of the Miwok diet.

Chumash Rock Painting

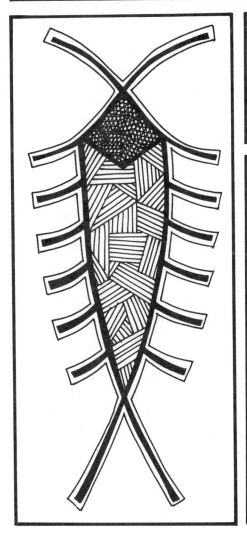

Finishing Touches

Make "rock paintings" by copying these designs on fine sandpaper with crayons. Most of the Chumash art was done in black, white, red, yellow, and orange.

Fascinating Facts

- Pictographs are Native American rock paintings found on rock surfaces such as caves and mountains.

- The Chumash Indians are known for producing colorful and elaborate pictographs.

- The Chumash mixed natural materials and oil to make paint for rock painting. The paint was applied to rock surfaces using the fingers or a brush made from an animal tail.

- Most pictographs in existence today are less than 2000 years old because the paint used to make them rarely survives the elements for periods of time longer than that.

Chumash Canoe

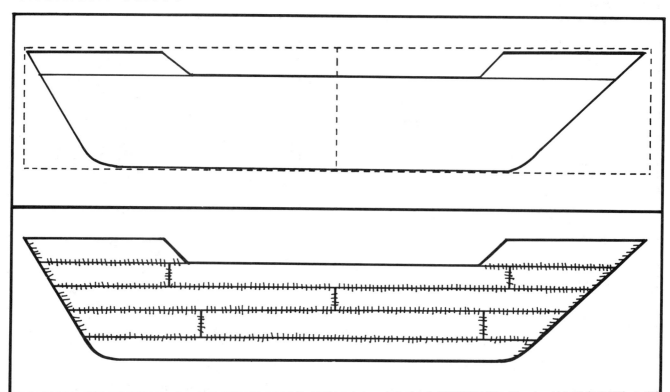

Finishing Touches
Draw yourself and a friend paddling a Chumash canoe. Decorate your canoe with pictures of a strong, brave animal, such as a bear or killer whale.

Fascinating Facts
- The Chumash lived along the California coast and on the three islands off the coast of Santa Barbara. Chumash depended on fish and sea mammals for their food.

- Chumash used tools made from shells, stones, and animal bones to make plank canoes. These canoes were called tomols.

- Tomols were built of planks cut from redwood trees. The planks were held together with tough cord made from milkweed string. A mixture of pine pitch and hardened asphalt called yop was used to fill the spaces between the planks.

- The tomols ranged from eight to thirty feet in length with the larger canoes holding as many as ten people.

La Brea Tar Pits

Mastodon statue in tar pit

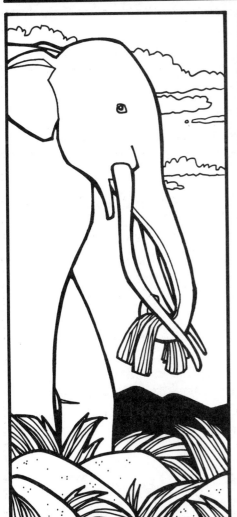

Finishing Touches

The plants that grew during the times of the mastodons were like those that we see today. Add grass and trees to the background of your picture, and draw some birds flying overhead.

Fascinating Facts

- The La Brea Tar Pits, located in Los Angeles, were discovered by Gaspar de Portolá in 1769.

- The tar pits oozed crude oil that thickened into pools of sticky black tar. Many prehistoric animals were trapped in the tar when they came to drink from the shallow water that covered the pools.

- The pits contain the fossilized skulls and bones of animals such as the mastodon, the mammoth, and saber-toothed cats. More than three million fossils have been found in the tar pits.

California Geodoodles
© The Learning Works, Inc.

Mission San Juan Capistrano

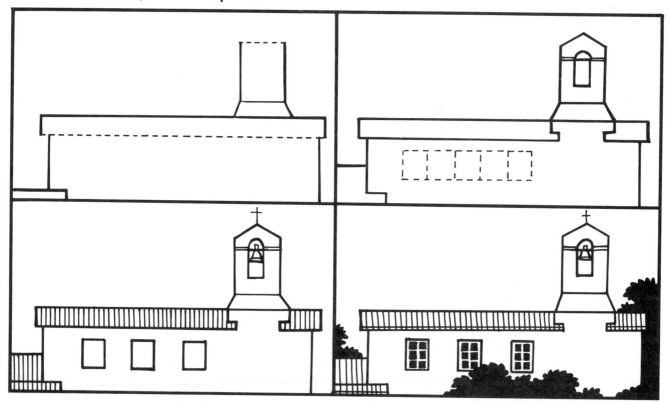

Finishing Touches
The mission is cream-colored with a red-orange tile roof. Draw clouds in the sky, and add a flock of swallows circling overhead.

Fascinating Facts

- Mission San Juan Capistrano was founded by Father Junípero Serra on November 1, 1776.

- Local Acagchemen Indians helped the Spanish soldiers and friars build the mission in exchange for food and trinkets.

- An earthquake destroyed much of the mission in 1812.

- Mission San Juan Capistrano is famous for the swallows that start arriving every March. The swallows have been returning to the mission every year since 1777.

Mission Santa Barbara

Finishing Touches
The mission is cream-colored, with red-orange domes atop its towers. The steps in front of the mission are golden tan. Design a postage stamp with a picture of this mission.

Fascinating Facts

- Mission Santa Barbara is often called the "Queen of the Missions." The mission is made from adobe.

- The mission was founded in 1786 and served as home to the Chumash Indians. Later missionaries lived in the mission.

- The mission complex included living quarters, kitchens, and gardens.

- The mission was destroyed by an earthquake on December 12, 1812 but was later rebuilt.

California Geodoodles
© The Learning Works, Inc.

Covered Wagon

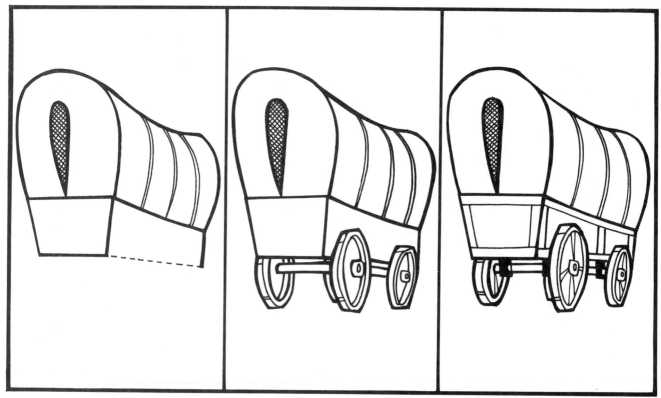

Finishing Touches
Some of the people heading west wrote messages on the canvas of their covered wagons, telling who they were, where they were going, and where they had come from. Write a message on your wagon.

Fascinating Facts
- Pioneers traveled to California in covered wagons in search of a better way of life.

- The wagons had broad, large wheels to make pulling easier for the oxen, mules, or horses. The ends of the covered wagon were higher than the middle to keep pioneer belongings and supplies from spilling or rolling.

- The top of the covered wagon could be closed or opened, depending on the weather.

- The covered wagons were strong and sturdy but not very comfortable. The average wagon could carry loads weighing up to six tons.

Sutter's Mill

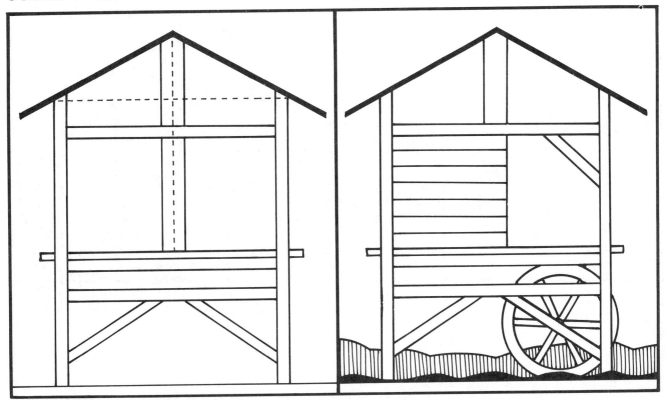

Finishing Touches

Draw a sawmill worker and his dog standing in the mill. Add tall evergreen trees and mountains in the background.

Fascinating Facts

- John Sutter owned a sawmill on the American River in the Sacramento Valley. The sawmill was about fifty miles from the large adobe fort John Sutter built as his headquarters.

- The mill was an open, wooden structure that was built over the river. Water turned a large wheel that moved a blade back and forth to cut the lumber at the mill.

- On January 24, 1848, gold was discovered at Sutter's Mill by James Wilson Marshall who was building a sawmill for John Sutter.

California Geodoodles
© The Learning Works, Inc.

Forty-Niner

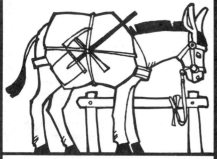

Finishing Touches

Blue jeans were developed during the gold rush. They were made by a man named Levi who saw that the miners needed tough pants to wear as they worked in the sand and gravel. Color your forty–niner's pants blue.

Fascinating Facts

- After gold was discovered at Sutter's Mill in 1848, news of gold spread to the eastern United States. Soon people with "gold fever" headed for California.

- Gold-rush miners were called forty-niners because they began their journey west to search for gold in 1849.

- Forty-niners panned for gold using a shallow metal pan. They put dirt and gravel from the river in their pan, added water, and swirled the pan around. The swirling motion sent the dirt and gravel flying out of the pan. Since gold is about seven times heavier than soil or gravel, the gold separated from the dirt and settled to the bottom of the pan.

Pony Express Rider

Draw the dotted lines first.

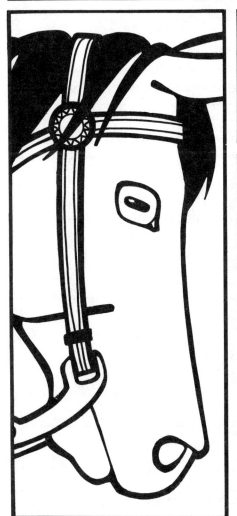

Finishing Touches

These riders delivered the mail through wild storms and intense heat. The terrain they crossed included woodlands, prairies, deserts, steep canyons, and level plains. Add a landscape around your horse and rider.

Fascinating Facts

- The Pony Express was a way of delivering mail by horse and rider relays between 1860 and 1861. The Pony Express route ran between St. Joseph, Missouri and Sacramento, California.

- It took riders about ten days to cover the 1,800-mile route. There were 157 stations on the route. Riders changed horses about six to eight times between stations.

- One of the most famous Pony Express riders was William Cody. He was known as Buffalo Bill.

- The Pony Express became obsolete with the introduction of the transcontinental telegraph on October 24, 1861. The Pony Express closed two days later.

California Geodoodles
© The Learning Works, Inc.

Stagecoach

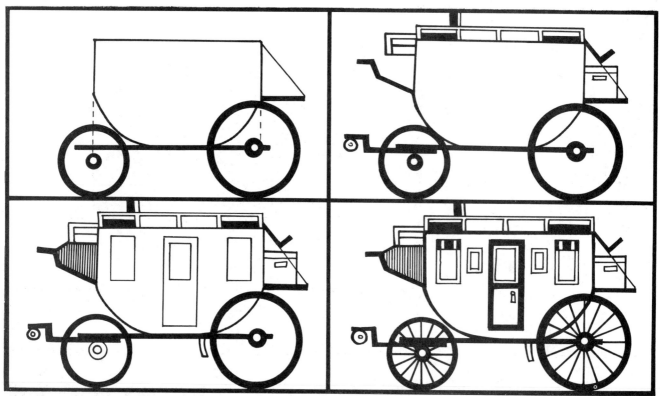

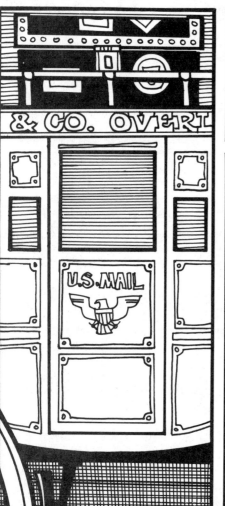

Finishing Touches

Above the windows and doors on the side of your coach, add a sign like the one below, or create a name for your own stage line. Write that name on your stagecoach.

WELLS FARGO & CO. OVERLAND STAGE

Fascinating Facts

- Stagecoaches were used to carry passengers, mail, and freight from the East to California.

- The stagecoaches were drawn by a team of horses. The horses were changed every fifteen or twenty miles at special relay stations that were set up along the route.

- Eventually railroads replaced stagecoaches because they provided a faster and more comfortable means of transportation.

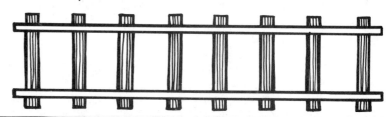

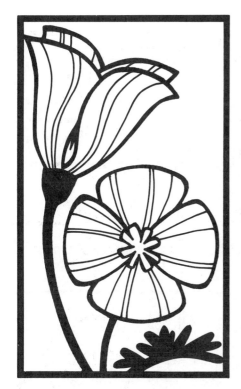

CALIFORNIA REPUBLIC

Landmarks & Symbols

Golden Gate Bridge

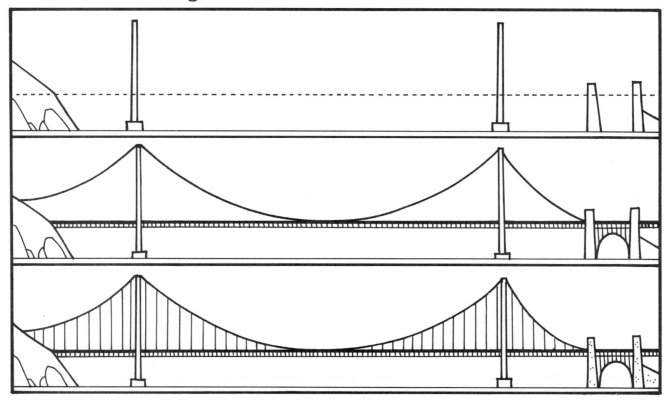

Finishing Touches

Add a sun, sailboats, and seagulls to your picture.

Fascinating Facts

• The Golden Gate Bridge is a suspension bridge that connects San Francisco with Marin County in northern California.

• The bridge is 8981 feet long, making it one of the longest single-span bridges in the world.

• The Golden Gate bridge is painted orange and is suspended from two cables hung from twin towers that are 746 feet high. It takes 5000 gallons of orange paint to cover the bridge.

• It took over four years and thousands of workers to build the bridge. The Golden Gate Bridge was completed in 1937.

Dragons' Gate

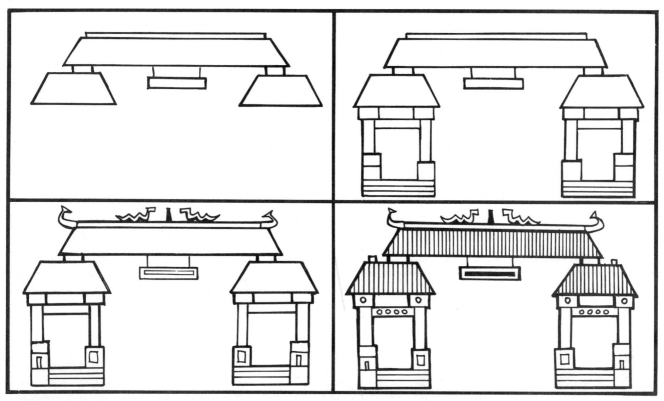

Finishing Touches

The gate's pillars are made from light gray stone, and the tile roof is green. The dragons are gold. Use your art to create a poster encouraging people to visit Chinatown.

Fascinating Facts

- The Dragons' Gate marks the main entrance to Chinatown in San Francisco.

- The Dragons' Gate was a gift from the Republic of China (Taiwan).

- The first Chinese arrived in San Francisco during the gold rush of 1849. Many settled in Portsmouth Square which later became Chinatown.

- Chinatown is a popular tourist spot because of all the colorful shops and restaurants.

25

Victorian House

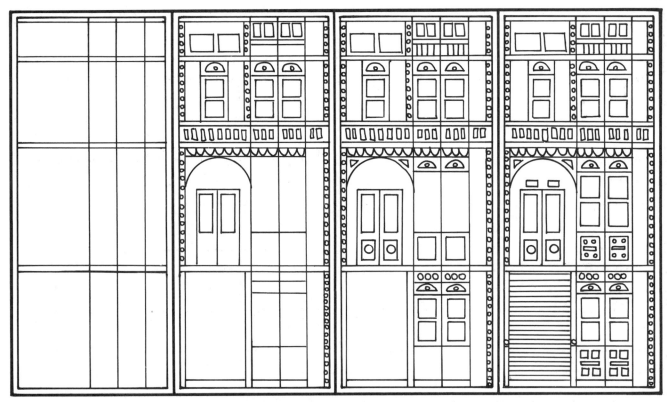

Finishing Touches

This drawing contains so much detail that it should be drawn on a large piece of paper—at least 7x16 inches. The houses are often painted in a rainbow of colors. Have fun coloring your house!

Fascinating Facts

- Victorian houses line the streets of San Francisco, Eureka, and other California cities.

- On the exterior many Victorian homes have distinctive gables, ornate trim, and elaborate balconies. Some homes have turrets or towers on top and columned porches that wrap around the house.

- On the interior many Victorian houses feature ornate fireplaces and claw-foot bathtubs.

Cable Car

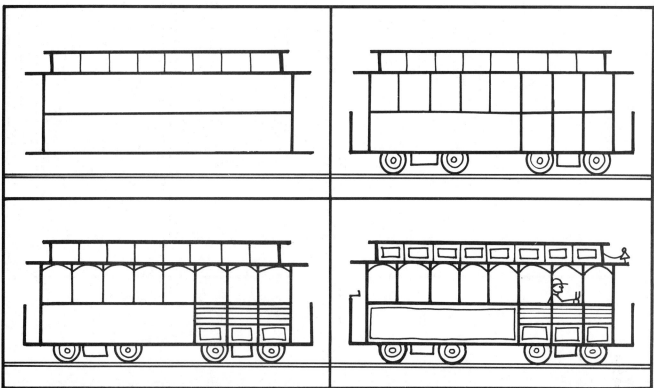

Finishing Touches

On the side of your cable car, draw a San Francisco landmark or create an ad for a restaurant or other attraction. If you wish, draw some passengers in your cable car.

Fascinating Facts

- Tourists who visit San Francisco can catch a ride on a cable car. The cable cars are ideal for running up and down the steep hills of the city.

- The cable car was invented by Andrew Hallidie, an American manufacturer. It was first used in San Francisco in 1873.

- The cars run along the street on tracks. They are pulled by a moving cable or steel rope. The cable car moves when the person operating the car pushes a lever. This causes the cable car's metal grip to latch onto the moving cable.

- Electric streetcars began to replace many of the cable cars in the 1890s.

Yosemite National Park

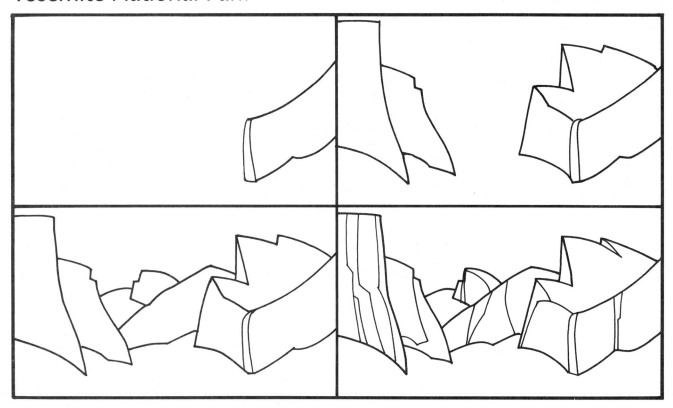

**Yosemite Falls
2,425 feet**

Finishing Touches

Yosemite Valley's floor is carpeted with green trees. The gray granite from which Yosemite is formed reflects pink or gold light at dawn and sunset. Consider drawing Yosemite as seen during a snowstorm or in moonlight.

Fascinating Facts

- Yosemite, located in east-central California, became a national park in 1890.

- Yosemite is famous for its beautiful giant sequoia groves. Many of the sequoia trees are thousands of years old. The tree known as the Grizzly Giant is more than 2700 years old.

- Yosemite National Park is home to many animals such as mule deer, black bears, chipmunks, and squirrels.

- Yosemite Falls is the highest waterfall in the United States.

Capitol Building

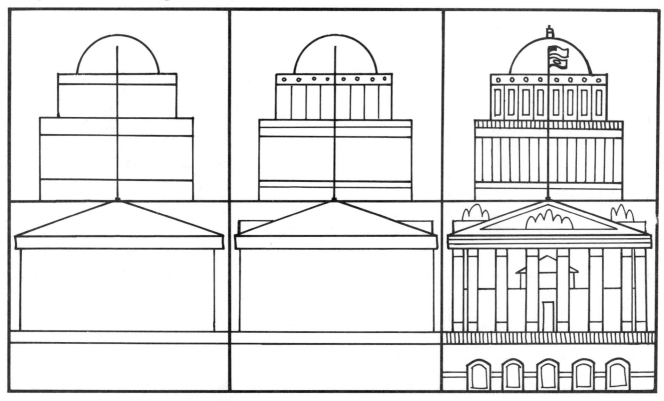

Finishing Touches

Draw the capitol building in the bottom half of a narrow strip of paper, leaving a large sky area. Then add a fireworks display.

Fascinating Facts

- California's state capitol building is in Sacramento.

- Sacramento has been the state capital since 1854. Before then the capital had temporarily been in five other cities between 1850 and 1854.

- The capitol building, completed in 1874, is topped with a small gold dome.

California Geodoodles
© The Learning Works, Inc.

Hearst Castle

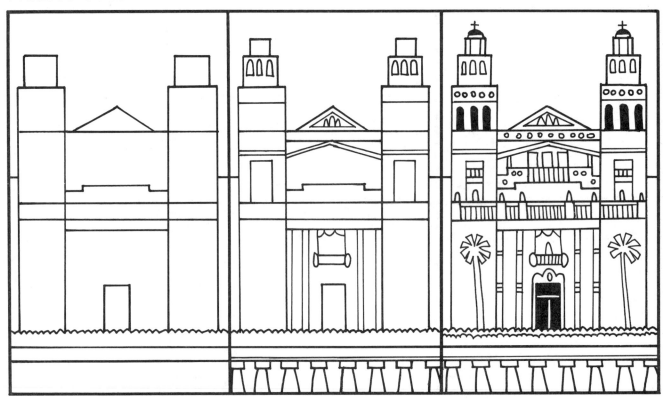

Finishing Touches

The many elaborate buildings of Hearst Castle are almost all white, with red roofs and areas of blue-and-yellow tile work.

Fascinating Facts

- Hearst Castle is built on 127 acres at San Simeon and overlooks the Pacific Ocean.

- Hearst Castle was the home of William Randolph Hearst, a newspaper publisher.

- There are 165 rooms including a theater and three guest houses on the property. The rooms are furnished with elegant treasures from palaces and churches of Europe.

Hollywood Sign

This drawing shows a six-foot-tall person standing on one of the sign's letters.

Finishing Touches

The Hollywood sign is white. Color the hillside green, and add a blue sky or a colorful sunset. You may wish to draw some seagulls, a blimp, or a helicopter flying past the sign.

Fascinating Facts

- The Hollywood sign is located on Mount Lee in Griffith Park in the Hollywood Hills.

- The original sign was built in 1923 and read "Hollywoodland."

- The current sign is 450 feet long, 50 feet tall, and weighs 450,000 pounds.

- The Hollywood sign was restored with all-steel letters and unveiled in 1978 to celebrate Hollywood's 75th anniversary.

- On January 1, 2000, this sign was the focal point of a huge Millennium celebration.

Death Valley

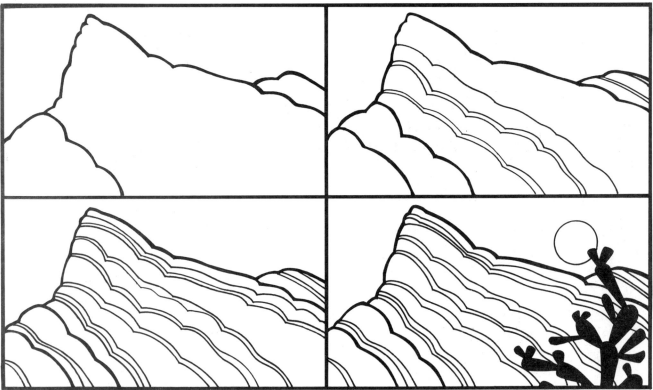

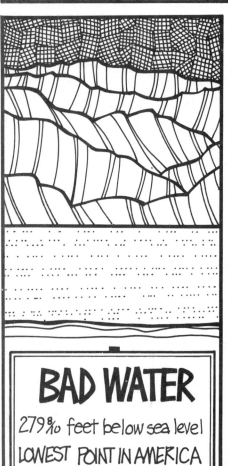

BAD WATER

279⁸⁄₁₀ feet below sea level
LOWEST POINT IN AMERICA

Finishing Touches

Earthquakes and volcanic activity have tilted and broken vast layers of rock in Death Valley. The tan and gray sandstone is streaked with minerals that tint it red, blue, green, or purple. Color the layers of rock in your picture.

Fascinating Facts

- Death Valley National Monument, home of Death Valley, is located near the Nevada border. The area only gets about two inches of rainfall a year.

- Death Valley got its name from the pioneers who made the dangerous journey across the 130-mile long valley in 1849. Many travelers died because they got lost or ran out of water.

- On July 10,1913, the temperature in Death Valley reached 134 degrees Fahrenheit and set a new record for the hottest temperature ever recorded in the United States.

Point Loma Lighthouse

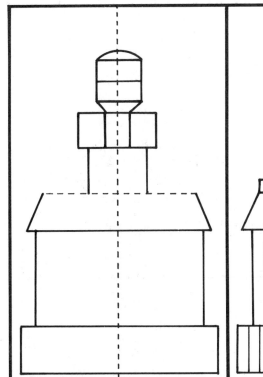

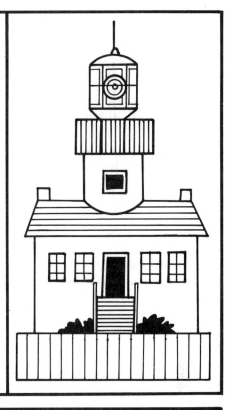

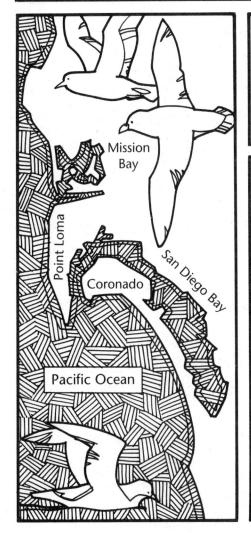

Finishing Touches
The lighthouse is white. Create a night sky or a colorful sunrise behind it. Use your art to design a stamp honoring lighthouses for guiding ships at sea and saving lives.

Fascinating Facts
- The original Point Loma Lighthouse, completed in 1854 and first lit in 1855, overlooks the San Diego Bay.

- Visitors to the lighthouse can climb a spiral staircase to view a special lens that was used to send out a beacon of light to sailors navigating the San Diego harbor.

- The original Point Loma Lighthouse was active until 1891. At that time a new lighthouse opened 100 yards south of the old one.

- The Cabrillo National Monument, located on the same site as the Point Loma Lighthouse, opened in 1913.

California Geodoodles
© The Learning Works, Inc.

Palomar Observatory

Draw the dotted lines first.

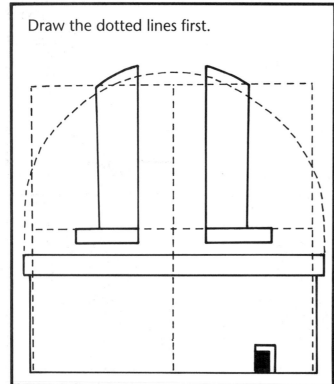

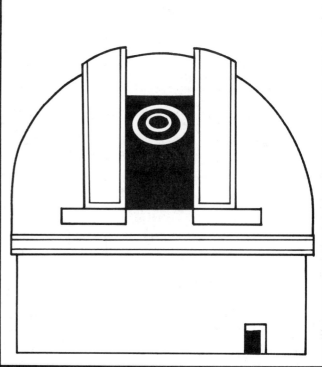

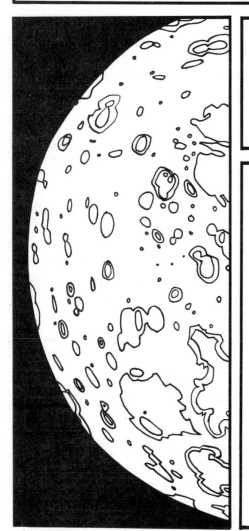

Finishing Touches

Try drawing the observatory on black paper using chalk or a pencil with white lead. Add your favorite constellation, a comet, or an eclipse to your drawing.

Fascinating Facts

- The Palomar Observatory is located in the mountains northeast of San Diego. It is home to the 200-inch Hale Telescope, one of the world's largest telescopes.

- The telescope was named for astronomer George Ellery Hale and was dedicated on June 3, 1948.

- Different parts of the telescope were constructed at sites all over the United States. They were then shipped to California and assembled inside a 135-foot tall dome. The telescope's 200-inch glass mirror was made from a glass blend called Pyrex and was constructed by Corning Glass Works in New York.

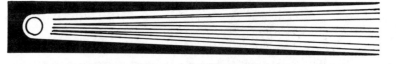

California Valley Quail (State Bird)

Finishing Touches

To find the exact coloration of this beautiful bird, look it up in a field guide. The female is protected by her duller coloration. Draw a pair of quail "parading" with their chicks.

Fascinating Facts

- The California Valley Quail is gray, brown, and gold with black and white markings.

- Quail are seed-eating birds that live on or near the ground in groups called coveys. One male stands guard while the other members of the covey feed.

- Quail chicks can run and feed themselves soon after they hatch.

- Most adult quail are 8 to 12 inches long.

California Geodoodles
© The Learning Works, Inc.

California Poppy (State Flower)

Finishing Touches
This flower varies in color from light yellow to deep orange. The leaves are lacy, like a carrot's, and are bluish or grayish green. Purple lupine flowers often share meadows and roadsides with these golden poppies.

Fascinating Facts
- The Golden Poppy, *Eschscholzia californica*, is often called the "cup of gold" and grows wild in California.

- In mid-April, fields and meadows in California's central valley are carpeted with these brightly-colored flowers.

- The Antelope Valley California Poppy Reserve is located in the high desert near Lancaster. At the reserve, 1745 acres have been set aside to protect and display the California poppy and other wildflowers.

Coast Redwood (State Tree)

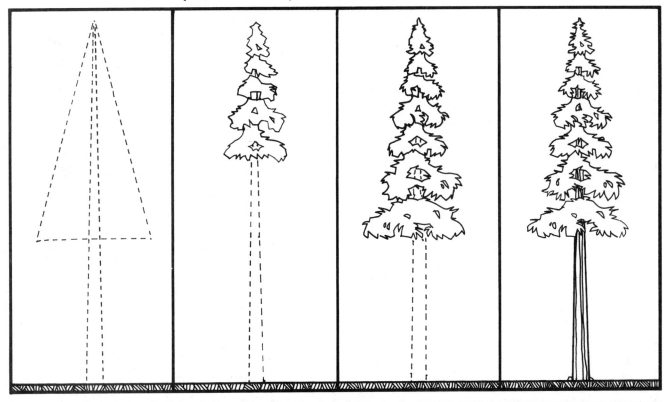

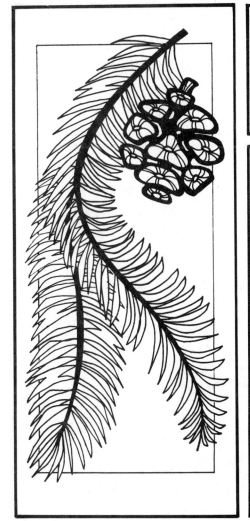

Finishing Touches

Try drawing a redwood tree on a piece of paper eight inches wide and thirty inches long. Each inch in the height of your drawing represents ten feet. Draw yourself standing next to the tree.

Fascinating Facts

- Redwoods grow in misty weather and can be found along the central and northern coast of California.

- Redwood trees are the tallest trees on earth. The average height of a redwood tree is between 200 and 275 feet but some have grown as tall as 368 feet.

- The Yurok tribe made its houses and canoes from strips cut from the redwood trees.

- Redwood seeds are about $1/16$ inch long. It would take about 123,000 seeds to make a pound.

California Geodoodles
© The Learning Works, Inc.

State Flag

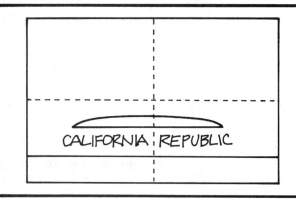

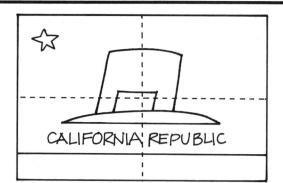

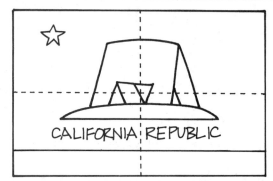

Finishing Touches

Color the stripe red. Color the bear brown. The bear is walking on green grass. The lettering is black. Leave the flag's background white.

California's state mammal, the grizzly bear

Fascinating Facts

- The California state flag was adopted in 1911.

- The flag features a red star, a red stripe, and a brown grizzly bear.

- The grizzly bear is California's state mammal.

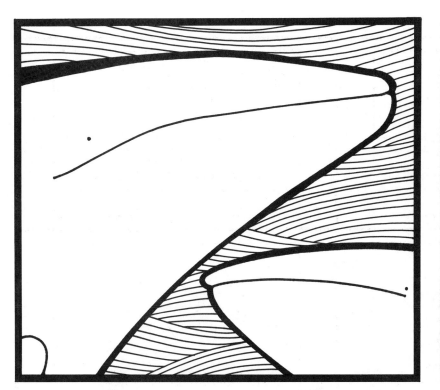
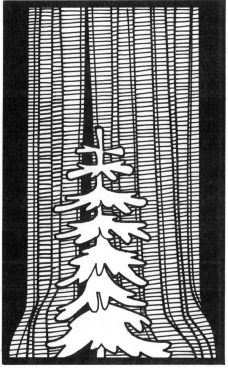

Animals & Plants

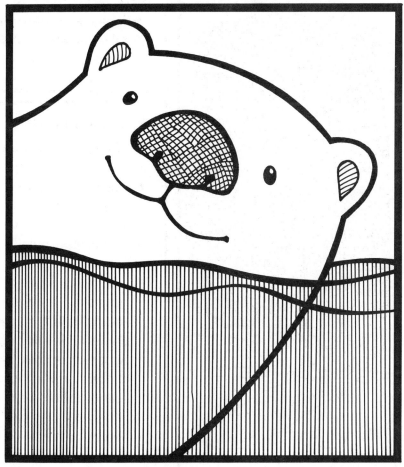

Sea Otter

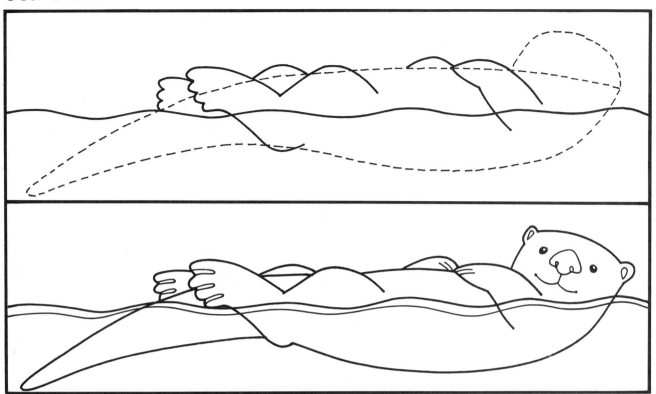

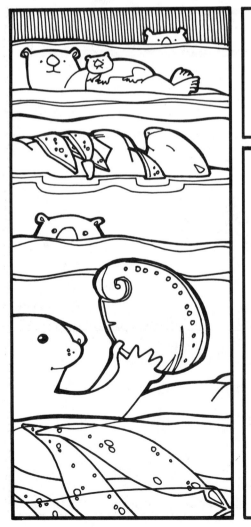

Finishing Touches

This otter has dark brown fur and a light tan face. It wraps seaweed around its body to keep from drifting as it sleeps. Draw a sleeping otter with seaweed wound around its belly.

Fascinating Facts

- There are approximately 2,000 sea otters along the coast of California from Santa Cruz to Point Conception.

- The sea otter is very playful and likes to sleep, rest, and swim on its back.

- The sea otter has the thickest fur of any mammal. It has as many as one million hairs per square inch. The sea otter has natural oils in its fur that repel water and trap tiny air bubbles. This provides a layer of warm air between the sea otter's skin and the water. This protection is important because sea otters do not have any blubber like other marine mammals do.

- Sea otters eat sea urchins, clams, crabs, and squid.

Gray Whale

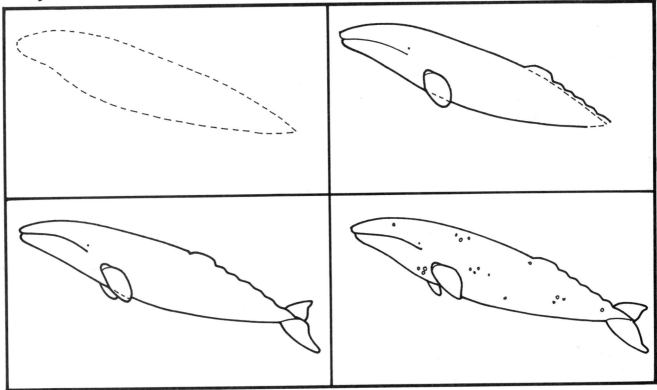

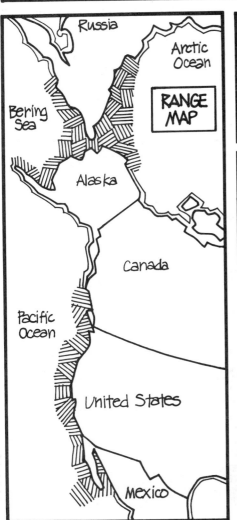

Russia
Arctic Ocean
Bering Sea
RANGE MAP
Alaska
Canada
Pacific Ocean
United States
Mexico

Finishing Touches

Baby whales are called calves. A newborn gray whale is about fifteen feet long—one-third the length of its mother. Draw a calf swimming next to your whale.

Fascinating Facts

- Gray whales make the longest migration of any mammal-sometimes more than ten thousand miles! They are easily seen from several points along the coast and may be seen up close from whale-watching boats.

- Curious and intelligent, gray whales often approach boats, sticking their heads up out of the water. This movement is called "spyhopping."

- A newborn gray whale is about fifteen feet long-about one third the length of its mother.

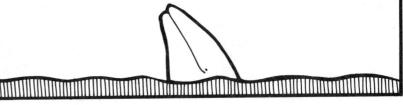

California Condor

Finishing Touches
The adult California condor is mostly black with a red-orange head and legs. There are bold white markings under the wings.

Fascinating Facts

- The California condor, the largest flying bird in North America, weighs up to 23 pounds and has a wingspan of up to $9\frac{1}{2}$ feet.

- The condor may live for fifty years or more.

- A female condor lays a single egg every other year.

- The condor is very rare and is endangered for several reasons—habitat destruction, slow reproduction, and environmental hazards.

Cliff Swallow

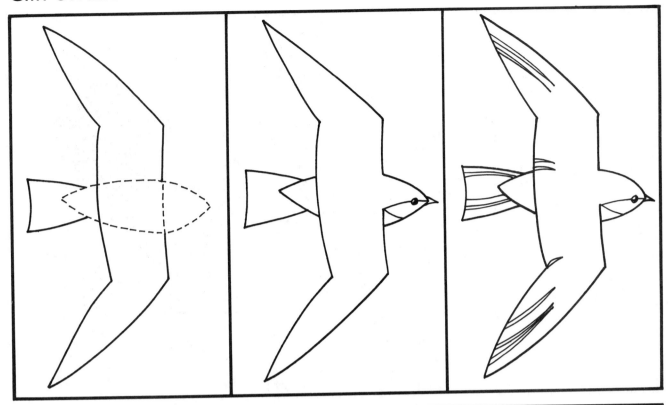

mud nest under eaves

swallows gathering mud

Finishing Touches

The top of this bird's head, wings, and tail are dark blue. The sides of its head are red. Its belly and back between the wings and tail are tan. Swallows catch flying insects. Draw a swallow chasing a moth or mosquito.

Fascinating Facts

- Cliff swallows build their nests under the roofs of the mission at San Juan Capistrano. Their nests are made out of balls of mud.

- The birds arrive from Argentina in mid March, build their nests, and raise their young. Then they fly to South America in October.

- The cliff swallows travel almost 6000 miles but always return to the mission in the spring.

Giant Sequoia

Finishing Touches
These huge trees have amazingly small roots. They grow in groves to support each other, weaving their roots together. This stabilizes them against storms. Draw a grove of sequoias with rust-red bark and green foliage.

Fascinating Facts

- Giant Sequoias grow high in the Sierra Mountains. Though not as tall as the coast redwoods to which they are related, they are far more massive. Some reach diameters of ten feet or more!

- The world's largest living thing is a giant sequoia tree named the General Sherman. It is found in Sequoia National Park.

- The General Sherman is between 2200 and 2500 years old. It is 275 feet tall and has a circumference of 103 feet.

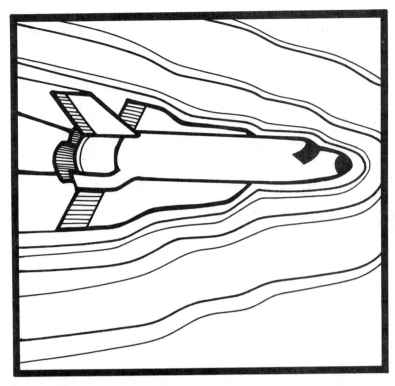

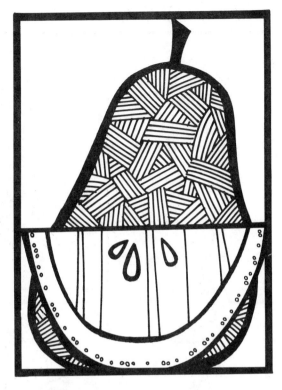

Business & Industry

Space Shuttle

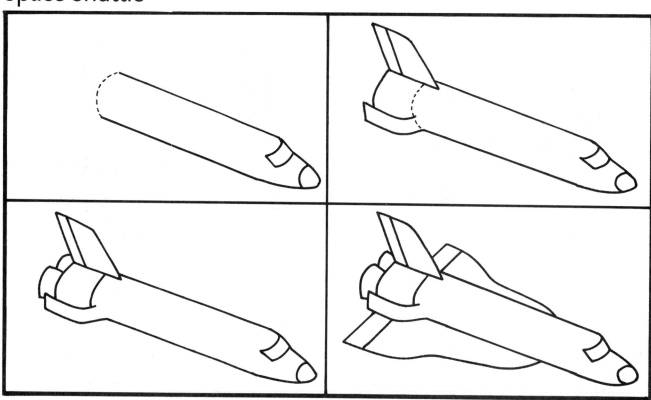

Finishing Touches
Cut a T-shirt shape from a large piece of paper. On it, design a shirt that might be worn by people watching the shuttle land at Edwards Air Force Base.

Fascinating Facts

- Space shuttle orbiters used by NASA are built in California. The shuttle orbiter can carry a crew of up to seven astronauts.

- Astronauts use the space shuttle to research and explore space. It is launched like a rocket and then orbits the earth like a spacecraft. The space shuttle lands on a runway at speeds between 213 to 226 miles per hour. Parachutes are used to help slow and steady the shuttle during its landing.

- The space shuttle sometimes lands at Edwards Air Force Base in California.

Oil Well

Finishing Touches

Use tracing paper or a copy machine to reproduce your drawing several times. Create a picture of an oil field with many wells.

Fascinating Facts

- In the 1800s, the most important oil strikes were in Los Angeles, Santa Barbara, and the San Joaquin Valley.

- On March 15, 1910, Charlie Woods discovered an oil gusher in the San Joaquin Valley. Over a period of eighteen months, his well ended up pumping more than nine million barrels of oil.

- The value of California's vast oil deposits is so great that this resource is sometimes called "black gold."

California Geodoodles
© The Learning Works, Inc.

Fishing Boat

Finishing Touches

The round objects on the side of the boat are floats which support the net when it is in the water. Their bright colors—hot pink, yellow, and neon orange—make them easy to spot at sea. Color your boat and floats.

Fascinating Facts

- Fishermen catch tuna, halibut, and marlin in the coastal waters of California.

- Tuna is the most profitable fish caught in California. More tuna is caught in California than in any other state.

- Popular shellfish found in the coastal waters of California include scallops, shrimps, oysters, clams, abalone, and crabs.

- Sturgeon, salmon, bass, catfish, and trout are some of the fish that can be found in California's rivers and freshwater lakes.

Movies

Finishing Touches

Fill in the silver screen with a scene from your favorite movie. Will it be a comedy, mystery, or action-packed adventure film?

Fascinating Facts

- In 1918 after World War I ended, Hollywood became very popular for the movie business.

- Silent movies were replaced by "talkies" in the late 1920s.

- Steamboat Willie, the first sound cartoon, was made in Hollywood in 1928 and featured Mickey Mouse.

- The California movie industry still attracts a lot of tourists who want to catch a glimpse of a movie star or tour a movie studio.

California Geodoodles
© The Learning Works, Inc.

California Crops

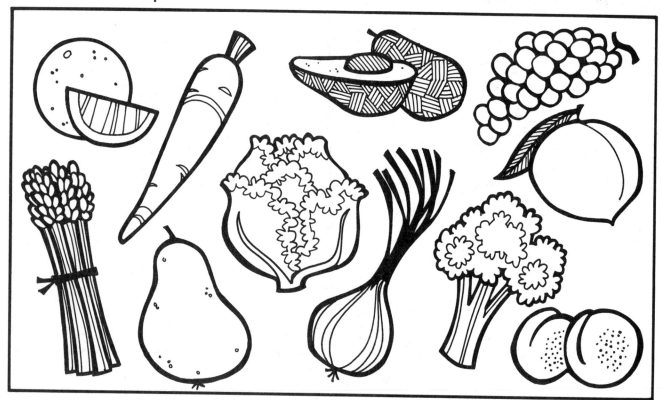

Finishing Touches

Using the fruits and vegetables you have drawn, design a cookbook cover or a banner for an outdoor farmers' market.

Fascinating Facts

- California is the nation's top agricultural state. About half of the fresh fruits and vegetables found in grocery stores in the United States are grown in California.

- California's sunny weather, rich soil, and good irrigation systems make it ideal for growing crops.

- Some of California's leading crops include asparagus, oranges, avocados, carrots, grapes, pears, peaches, apricots, broccoli, onions, and lettuce.

Sports&Recreation

Wind Surfer

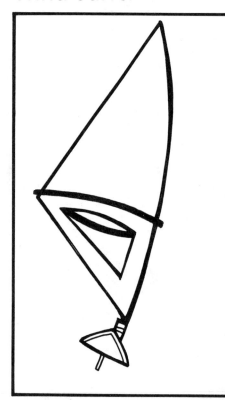

Finishing Touches

The sails on these boards are usually brightly colored with bold patterns and designs. Draw yourself wind surfing, and design a personalized sail for the board you are riding.

Fascinating Facts

- Wind surfing is a sport that combines sailing and surfing.

- Wind surfers operate a one-person craft known as a sailboard.

- The first sailboard models were created in the 1950s. In 1968 two Californians, Jim Drake and Hoyle Schweitzer, obtained a patent for a sailboard design known as the Windsurfer.

- Early sailboards could only reach moderate speeds and had to be used near shore, but recent specialized sailboards have reached speeds of 40 knots and have sailed across the Atlantic Ocean.

Skateboarder

Finishing Touches
Draw your skateboarder in a half pipe or quarter pipe. You might want to add some extra action by turning your drawing sideways or upside down before finishing the picture.

Fascinating Facts

- Skateboarding originated in California in the 1930s and became popular in southern California in the 1960s.

- Skateboarding became even more popular in the 1970s with the development of the faster, easier to maneuver polyurethane wheel.

- Some of the freestyle stunts used in skateboarding include "wheelies," "ollies," and "kickturns."

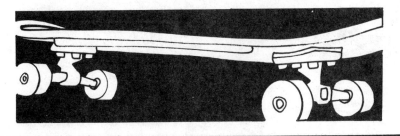

Scuba Diver

Finishing Touches
These fishes are found along the California coast. Add some to your drawing of the scuba diver.

Fascinating Facts

- The word scuba is an acronym for the words self-contained underwater breathing apparatus.

- Scuba diving began in 1943 when the first gear was developed.

- Scuba divers bring back useful information about fish and other marine life. They also explore ships that have sunk and collect information on water pollution.

Mountain Climber

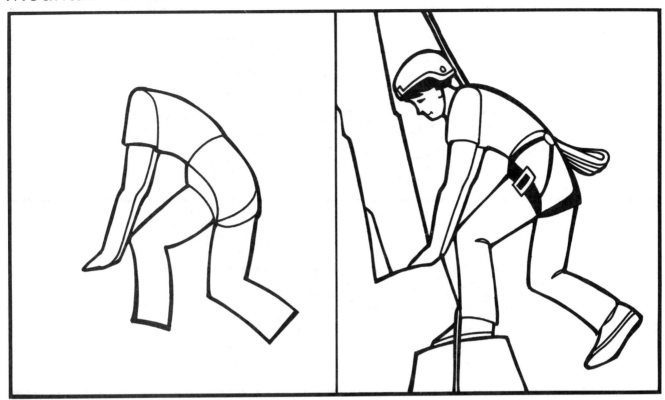

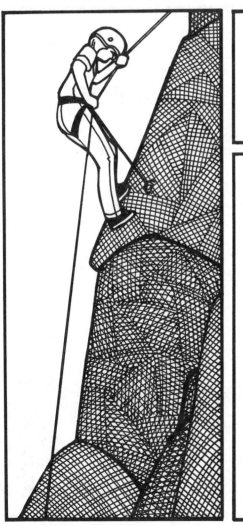

Finishing Touches

Create a more exciting picture by drawing on a long, narrow piece of paper. Put some clouds in the sky, and add mountain peaks far below your climber.

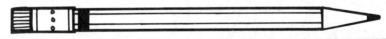

Fascinating Facts

• Mountain climbers must be good hikers and rock climbers. They must also be in excellent physical shape.

• Mountain climbers use ropes, special shoes, and other equipment to climb and almost always climb with a partner.

• In 1970, climbers scaled the 3000 foot smooth granite face of El Capitan in Yosemite National Park. It took them twenty-seven days to make the climb.

• Mt. Whitney is the highest point in the forty-eight contiguous states.

Skier

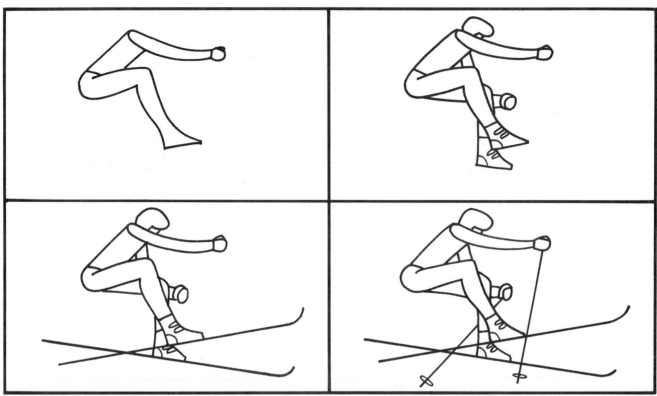

Finishing Touches

Make a large drawing of your skier on a sheet of poster board. Add colorful designs to your skier's outfit. If you wish, turn your art into a poster for your favorite ski area or resort.

Fascinating Facts

- California's mountain ranges provide many excellent locations for both downhill and cross-country skiing.

- Some of the places noted for good skiing include Mount Baldy, Mammoth Mountain, Mount Shasta, Badger Pass, and Big Bear Mountain.

- One of the largest ski areas in the United States is Squaw Valley, located in the Sierras. Squaw Valley was home to the 1960 Winter Olympic Games.

Special Events

Chinese New Year Dragon

Finishing Touches
Try making a long dragon on a narrow strip of paper. Use many bright colors as you decorate it. In China, red is the favorite color for happy holiday costumes and decorations.

Fascinating Facts
- Chinese New Year is celebrated between January 21 and February 19.

- The Chinese New Year ends with a festive parade led by a long dragon. The dragon is believed to chase away bad luck.

- The dragon is made of bamboo, paper, and silk. People hold the dragon up and dance through the streets.

Jazz Musician

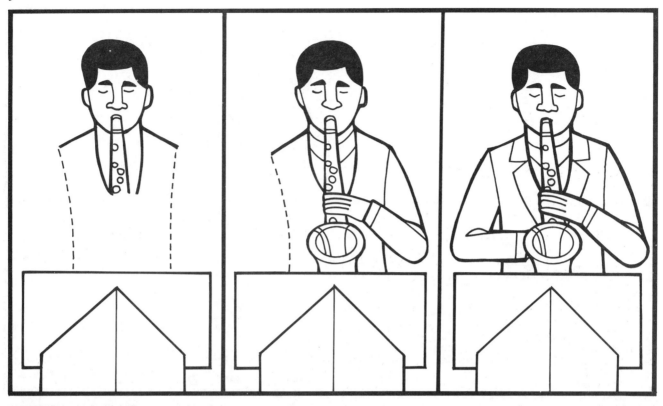

Finishing Touches
Think of a catchy name for a jazz band, and write it on a banner over your musician's head. Decorate the music stand with a colorful design.

Fascinating Facts
- Jazz festivals are held each year in many California cities such as Monterey, Ojai, Santa Barbara, and Sacramento.

- Jazz music can be performed by solo musicians, a small group of musicians called a combo, or by a group featuring ten or more musical instruments called a big band.

- The folk songs and music of early African Americans contributed a great deal to early jazz music.

59

Rose Parade Float

BOOKS ARE FUN TO SHARE ANYWHERE • VISIT YOUR LIBRARY!

Finishing Touches

Rose parade floats are designed to honor cities, people, service groups, and great accomplishments. They carry educational and encouraging messages. Design a float that would honor a person or group that you admire.

Fascinating Facts

- Every New Year's Day, beautiful floats decorated with flowers can be found in the Tournament of Roses Parade in Pasadena.

- Some of the floats are more than fifty feet long. People spend days attaching fresh roses and other flowers to the floats. Some floats take as long as a year to construct.

- All surfaces of the float must be covered with some form of plant material such as flowers, leaves, petals, bark, or seeds. Each float is decorated with more flowers than the average florist will use in five years!

Calaveras Jumping Frog

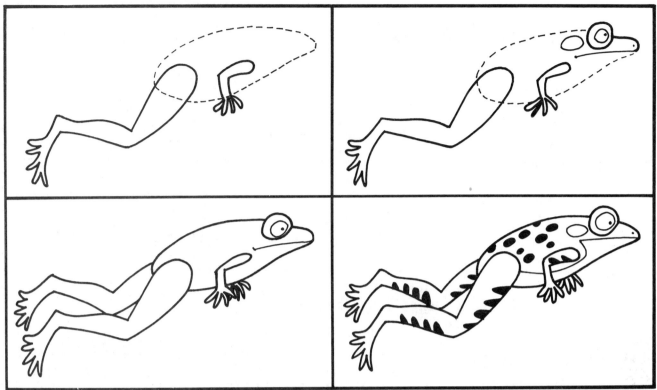

Finishing Touches
Color your frog dark green or greenish-brown with a white belly. Color the eye gold. You may wish to draw a group of frogs all jumping forward, or just one frog leaping to catch a fly.

Fascinating Facts

• Each year in May, the town of Angels Camp in Calaveras County, north of Modesto, hosts The Calaveras Country Fair and Jumping Frog Jubilee.

• The contest gets its name from a story written by Mark Twain called "The Celebrated Jumping Frog of Calaveras County."

• Prizes are given to the owners of the frogs that can jump the greatest distances. The world record for the longest jump was set in May 1986 when Rosie the Ribiter jumped 21 feet, 5.75 inches.

• Qualifying trials are held daily during the fair and the top fifty frogs advance to the grand finals for a chance to win the title.

California Geodoodles
© The Learning Works, Inc.

Creative Ways
to Use *California Geodoodles*

Design a Postage Stamp
Pretend you have been selected to design a postage stamp in honor of California. On a sheet of white art paper, design a stamp that includes one or more of the Geodoodles. Include a number that tells the value of the stamp. Color your design.

Tall Tales or Legends
Select a plant or animal from the California Geodoodles. Write a tall tale about a special feature of the plant or animal you selected. Here are some ideas to get you started:

- How the Redwood Trees Got So Tall
- How the Sea Otter Got Its Name
- Why the Swallows Return to Capistrano

3-D Gray Whale
Draw the gray whale found on page 41 on a large sheet of white butcher paper that has been folded in half as shown. Cut out your drawing so you end up with two copies. Staple all around the edges except for the bottom. Color both sides of your gray whale. Then stuffed crumpled-up newspapers inside your whale so it puffs out. Finish stapling the bottom part of the whale so the newspapers don't fall out. Hang your 3-D gray whale in your room using string or colored yarn.

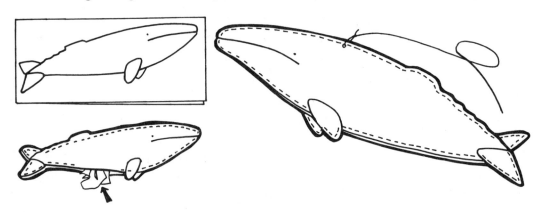

Make a Collage
Make a collage on white art paper comprised of your favorite Geodoodles. Draw each Geodoodle on a separate piece of paper. Include drawings from each section of the book so you have representative pictures from California's history, landmarks, symbols, plants, animals, businesses, sports, and special events. After your pictures are drawn, color them with colored marking pens, crayons, or colored pencils. Arrange them on a larger sheet of paper to make an interesting collage. Add words that make you think of California.

Creative Ways
to Use *California Geodoodles*

Note Cards
Make personalized note cards to send to your friends and relatives using your favorite California Geodoodle drawing. Just draw and color the design on white, unlined index cards or white art paper.

Make a Magnet
Turn your favorite California Geodoodle design into a magnet. Draw your design on white cardboard, cut it out, and color it with colored marking pens. Glue a small magnet to the back. (Magnets are available in most craft stores.) Make a whole set of magnets to give as gifts for the holidays or for special occasions.

California Concentration Game
Pick eight drawings from the California Geodoodle book. Using 3" x 5" unlined index cards, draw and color two identical images of each of the eight designs you select. Pick a name for your game such as "Pick a Pair" or "California Concentration". Write this name on the back of the sixteen index cards. Design and add a logo. Decorate the outside of a box in the theme you selected, and place your cards in the box. Give your boxed game to a younger child to play where they try to find matching pairs of Geodoodles.

Geodoodle Name Tags
California Geodoodles are ideal for name tags when you go on a field trip or have a guest or a substitute teacher in your class. They can also be used to place on your desk for Back-to-School Night or for school open houses. Just pick your favorite design in the book and draw it on white art paper. Color your drawing, and cut it out. Add your name in large letters inside the image.

Three Tricky Statements
Pick one of the California Geodoodle topics you'd like to learn more about. Browse the Internet and use reference materials to find twelve fascinating facts about the topic. Write each fact on a separate index card. Then make up three false statements about your topic. Write one false statement per card. Number your fifteen index cards mixing the false statements in with the true facts. Put the cards in an envelope and see if a friend can pick out which three statements are false.

California Decorative Borders

San Francisco

SAN DIEGO

YOSEMITE

CARMEL

CALIFORNIA!